Contents

Welcome to The Rise and Shine Museum

1 **Look, think and write.** | museum director~~ exhibitions app camera phone

1 I'm Eva. I'm the <u>museum director</u>.

2 I'm _____. There's a museum _____ on my tablet.

3 I'm _____. I like the cat.

4 I'm _____, the museum cat.

5 I'm _____. I've got a _____

and a _____.

6 I'm _____. I like _____.

Tell me!
Which of the Rise and Shine characters do you like?

2 🎧 0.08 **Listen, circle and write.**

1 a 16th   b (15th)   c 14th   3 a 5th   b 4th   c 3rd

2 a 1st   b 11th   c 21st   4 a 2nd   b 12th   c 22nd

5 The Museum Open Day is on the _____ of November.

3 💬 **When are the birthdays? Look and write. Then ask and answer.**

①  ②  ③  ④

1 It's on the <u>1st</u> of <u>October</u>.   3 It's on _____.

2 It's on the _____ of _____.   4 _____

> *When's your birthday?*   *It's on the 1st of October.*

Extra time? When is your birthday? Tell your friends.

4 Read and write.

1 We've __got__ tablets. We __can__ go online.

2 We've _____ the app. We _____ use the map.

3 We've _____ cameras. _____ take photos.

4 _____ phones. _____ make films.

Let's build!
What have we got and what can we do?

5 Look. Ask and answer. Then tell the class.

1 SCIENCE

2 ADVENTURE TIME SOS

3

4 AGE 9-11 VOLCANO SURFER PRO 2 PLAYERS!

5

science books   storybooks   toy cars   computer games   holiday photos

Do you like science books?

Yes, I do.

Me, too! We both like science books!

I can shine!

6 Imagine a time capsule for your family. Think and write. Then ask and answer.

My BLOG

HOME | NEWS | KID REPORTER | SHARING | FUN TIMES

In my family, we like _____ and _____ .
We like _____ , too.

We've got a / an _____ and _____
in our family time capsule.

We've also got _____ .

What have you got in your family time capsule?

We've got holiday photos in our family time capsule. We like the beach.

Extra time? Do you like museums?

Who are we?

Let's review! `PB p4–5`

Think and write.

1 `p a p` *a p p*   3 `s u m m u e` _____

2 `n p o h e` _____   4 `a c m a e r` _____

1 Read and number.

`1` curly hair	☐ straight hair	☐ wavy hair	☐ blonde hair	☐ big eyebrows
☐ beard	☐ moustache	`1` freckles	☐ ponytail	☐ smile

2 Look at Activity 1 and write.

1 She's got <u>curly hair</u> and <u>freckles</u>.

2 She's got _____ hair and a big _____.

3 He's got _____ hair, glasses and a _____.

4 He's got big _____ and a brown _____.

5 She's got _____ hair and a long _____.

Tell me!

Which are similar: blonde hair, black hair, dark hair and fair hair?

Extra time? What's similar about the people in the picture in Activity 1?

1 🎧 (1.06) **Listen and write.**

1 She's __got__ freckles. She __hasn't got__ a smile.

2 She _____ a big smile.

3 He _____ a beard.

4 He's _____ big _____ but he _____ a moustache.

5 She's _____ and a _____ but she _____ curly _____ .

2 💬 **What do they look like? Match. Then ask and answer.**

①

②

a She hasn't got a smile. ☐

b She hasn't got freckles. ☐

c She hasn't got curly hair. 1

d She hasn't got a ponytail. ☐

What does she look like?

She's got curly hair. She hasn't got dark hair.

I can shine! ✳

3 💬 **Write notes about a family member or friend. Then ask and answer.**

What does your person look like?

He's / She's got _____ and _____ . He / She hasn't got _____ .

Extra time? Write new words in their word families. Draw a picture for each word.

1 **Look and match. Then circle.**

a My special thing is a **drum** / **blanket**.

b My special thing is a **coin** / **bracelet**.

c My special thing is a **necklace** / **drum**.

d My special thing is **chocolate** / **a bracelet**.

2 **Read the story again. Then number.**

a **1**   b ☐   c ☐   d ☐

I can **shine!**

Let's imagine!
What do you think?
The story is: OK ☆   good ☆☆
great ☆☆☆

3 **Imagine you've got a special thing from the story. Write.**

I've got the _____ from the story.

It's _____ and _____.

I think it's _____.

Extra time? What's your special thing? Can you see, hear or smell it?

1 **Look and write.**

1 Has he got a blanket?

No, _he hasn't_ . He has got a _football_ .

2 Has she got a drum?

No, _____.
She _____ a guitar.

3 _____ she got a necklace?

Yes, _____.

4 _____ earrings?

_____ She _____ glasses.

Let's build!
What has your friend got on his / her desk?

I can **shine!**

2 **What is your special thing? Write and say.**

1 Look! This is my _____ thing. It's _____.

2 Sorry, I _____ understand. _____ you _____?

3 _____ of course. This is my _____. Look!

Pronunciation Circle the odd word out: café gallery coin camera computer coat

1 **Read and match.**

① I always read books.

② I often play my drum.

③ I sometimes take photos.

④ I never play my sister's guitar.

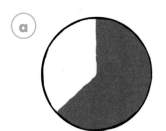
ⓐ

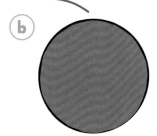
ⓑ

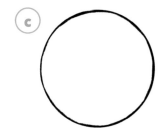
ⓒ

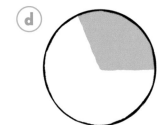
ⓓ

2 🎧 **1.17 Listen and number. Then write.**

ⓐ ☐

ⓑ 1

ⓒ ☐

ⓓ ☐

1 I ___always___ play my drum after school.

2 I _____ kick my football with my friends.

3 I _____ play my guitar for my family.

4 I _____ use my blanket in summer!

Think about something that is important to everyone. Why is it important?

3 **Write for you. Use *always*, *often*, *sometimes* and *never*.**

1 I _____ brush my teeth.

2 I _____ forget my books.

3 I _____ play chess.

4 I _____ make films.

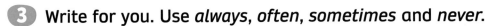

Extra time? How many children in your class have got brown eyes? Count.

1 Read, look and circle. What is Pippa's special thing?

A special present

My special thing is a present from my granny. She's very important to me. I ¹(**often**)/ **never** talk to her on the phone.

I'm ²**always** / **sometimes** happy when I use my special thing. I ³**always** / **never** use it when it's hot. I ⁴**sometimes** / **always** share it with my sister. What is it? Yes, it's my blanket. It's very special to me.

Pippa, 9, Ireland

SEARCH

2 Give it a go 💬 **Complete for you. Then ask and answer.**

My special thing		
	You	Your friend
What's your special thing?		
What does it look like? Is it old / new / big / small?		
Why is it important?		

I can shine!

3 Write about your friend's special thing. Use your notes from Activity 2.

My friend's special thing is _____.

It is _____.

It's important to him / her because _____.

He / She often / sometimes / always / never _____

_____.

Check your work! Check your friend's writing. Is the spelling correct?

1 Look and complete. Which word is missing in the puzzle?

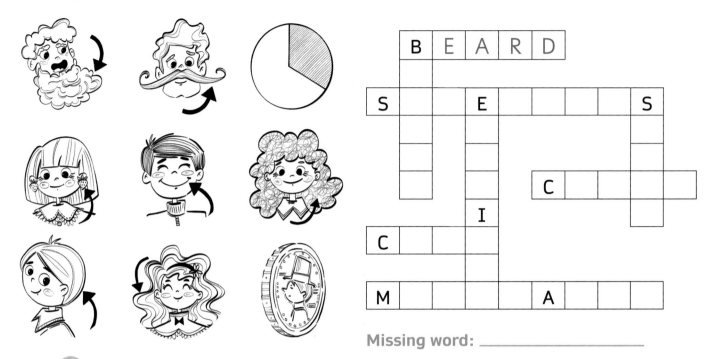

	B	E	A	R	D			

| S | | | E | | | | S |

| | | | C | | |

| | | I | | |

| C | | |

| M | | | | A | | | |

Missing word: _____

2 🎧 1.20 Listen and circle Holly's uncle. Then listen again and write.

💬 **BLOG** 🔍

Holly's uncle ¹ _has_ got straight,

dark ² _____.

He ³ _____ got a moustache

and he ⁴ _____ a ⁵ _____.

He ⁶ _____ glasses.

He ⁷ _____ got a white T-shirt.

3 Think and write.

◁ *This is my mum's necklace.*

Sorry, I ¹ _don't understand_ . ▷

◁ *Yes,* ³ _____.
This is my ⁴ _____.

Can ² _____
_____, *please?* ▷

Extra time? People wear them in their ears. They're... .

1 **Think about three special people. Complete. Use the words or your own ideas.**

> ponytail   bracelet   blonde   straight   curly   wavy
> dark   moustache   drum   freckles   earrings

Name	Features			Special thing
mum	blonde hair	ponytail	freckles	old bracelet

2 **Make your lapbook. Find pictures or draw. Then write.**

My special person

1 What does your special person look like? _____

2 What are his / her special things? _____

3 How often does he / she use them? _____

Home-school link 📎 Tell your family about your special people and things.

11

Let's use it again!

Let's review! PB p10–11

Think and write *face* or *hair*.

1 curly   _hair_   4 ponytail _____

2 blonde _____   5 smile _____

3 freckles _____   6 beard _____

Lesson 1 ➡ Vocabulary

1 **Read and number.**

☐ bowl   ☐ plate   ☐ rug   ☐ shelf   ☐ sweater

☐ cup   ☐ box   ☐ pot   ☐1 jacket   ☐ handbag

GIFT SHOP

2 **Look and write.**

1 This is a _box_ and this is a _plate_.

2 That's a handbag and that's a _____.

3 There are four _____ and there's a _____.

4 There are two _____ and there's a _____.

> **Tell me!**
> *Which things in your classroom can you upcycle? What can you make?*

 12

Extra time? Look at Activity 1. Which things have you got at home? Tell your friend.

1 (2.06) Listen and tick (✓) or cross (✗). Then listen again and write.

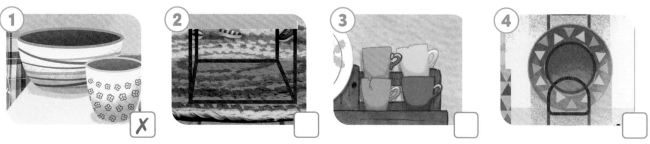

1 I _don't_ want _these_ bowls.

2 I want _____ rug.

3 I want _____ cups.

4 I _____ want _____ plate.

2 (2.07) Look and match. Then listen and check. Point and say.

1 Those jackets are

2 These sweaters are

3 Those handbags are

4 That sweater is

5 This handbag is

on the wall.

on the table.

on the shelf.

Those jackets are on the wall.

I can shine!

3 Look at Activity 2. Choose, think and write.

cute   beautiful   old   new   big
small   this / that   these / those

I like this _handbag_ because it's _cute_ .

I don't like those _____ because they're _____ .

I like _____ because _____ .

I don't _____ because _____ .

Extra time? Practise saying the new words.

13

1 **Look and write. Tick (✓) the sentences from the story. Then listen and check.**

plastic   paper   rubber   glass

1   This is a beautiful
glass bowl. ☐

2   I like this _____
boot. ☐

3   There are some
_____ cups and
some _____ plates. ☐

2 **Look and number.**

a ☐   b ☐   c 1   d ☐

1   The children think about the problem.
2   It's a new flower pot!
3   The children want to do some upcycling.
4   They find some interesting things.

I can shine!

Let's imagine!
What do you think? The story is:
OK ☆   good ☆☆   great ☆☆☆

3 **What can the children upcycle? Think and write.**

| rubber boot   plastic cup   paper plate
metal pot   wood   glass bowl |
|---|

They can use the _wood_ to make a _table_ .
They can use the _____ to make a _____ .
They can use the _____ to make a _____ .
They can use the _____ to make a _____ .

Extra time? Socks wants a new bed. What can he use to sleep in?

1 **Look and write.** mine   yours   his   hers

1 These rubber boots are _mine_ .

2 That metal necklace is _____ .

3 These plastic cups are _____ .

4 This glass bowl is _____ .

Let's build!

Play a game in a group. Use your things. Ask and answer.

2 (2.16) **Read and circle. Then listen and check.**

1 **Would** / **Can** you **want** / **like** to come to my picnic on Sunday?

2 Yes, **please** / **thanks**. I'd love to!

3 No, **please** / **thanks**. Sorry, I can't.

I can shine!

3 **Choose a day for your party. Then ask and answer.**

Monday	Tuesday	Wednesday	Thursday	Friday	Saturday	Sunday

Would you like to come to my party on Friday?

Yes, please. I'd love to!

No, thanks. Sorry, I can't.

Pronunciation Say. Then put the words into two groups: love cup party can't rug glass

1 Read and match.

 ①  ②  ③  ④

a It's a vegetable garden. It uses an ugly car.

b It's a huge giant. It uses old wood.

c It's a cute flower pot. It uses a little cup.

d It's a pretty garden. It uses an old bicycle.

2 2.20 Listen and number. Then write. Listen again and check.

| huge | ~~little~~ | pretty | ugly |

    ⒈

a It's an _____ sweater.

b It's a _____ handbag.

c It's a _____ jacket.

d It's a _____little_____ necklace.

3 Write for you.

1 I think my _____ is / are pretty.

2 I don't think my _____ is / are ugly.

3 My _____ is / are little.

4 My _____ is / are huge.

Do people upcycle rubbish in your country?

Extra time? How can you upcycle your rubbish?

1 **Read and answer. *True* or *false*?**

1 The party is for the exhibition. <u>True</u>

2 Everyone can come to the party. _____

3 The party is on Tuesday. _____

4 You must bring something old. _____

There's a party at the museum for our 'Old and new' exhibition. Everyone welcome.

Where? It's at The New Town Museum.

When? It's on Thursday at four o'clock.

Please bring something old or new to put in our exhibition.

2 Give it a go **Plan an exhibition party invitation. Make notes.**

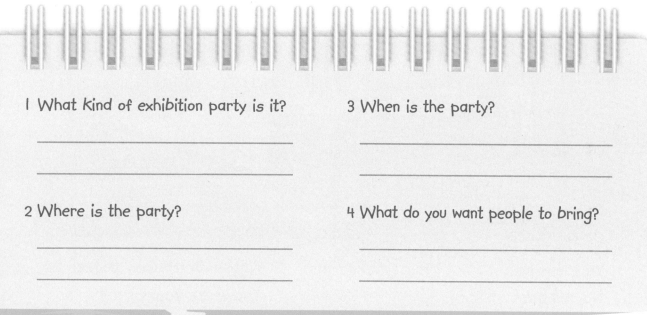

1 What kind of exhibition party is it?

_____

_____

2 Where is the party?

_____

_____

3 When is the party?

_____

_____

4 What do you want people to bring?

_____

_____

I can shine!

3 **Write your exhibition party invitation.**

Please come to: _____

Where? _____

When? _____

Please bring: _____

MUSEUM

Check your work! Order the letters. Write. cketaj rrbbue trawees ssgal eugh itllte

1 **Think and complete.**

> ~~paper~~ plastic cup sweater ~~glass~~ plate rug handbag

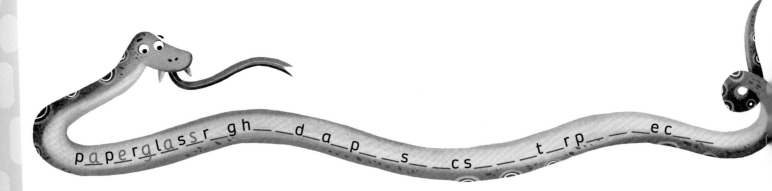

p a p e r g l a s s r _ g h _ _ _ d _ a _ p _ _ _ s _ _ c s _ _ _ _ t _ r p _ _ _ _ e c _ _ _ _

2 (2.23) **Listen and circle. Then write. Listen again and check.**

1 Whose is that __box__ ? Is it (**yours**) / **his**?
No, it's **hers** / **his**.

2 Whose are **these** / **those** _____?
They're **his** / **hers**.

3 Whose are **these** / **those** _____?
Those are **yours** / **hers**, too.

4 Whose is **this** / **that** _____?
That's **mine** / **yours**.

3 **Think and write.**

> ¹ _Would you like to_ come to
> my birthday party?

Yes, ² _____.
I'd ³ _____.

No, ⁴ _____.
Sorry, ⁵ _____.

Extra time? You can't put things in this. Is it a box, a rug, a pot or a cup?

1 🖊 **Think and write.**

paper

glass

cup
_____

metal
_____
_____

_____
_____

_____
_____

rubber

wood

plastic

_____

_____
_____

_____
_____

_____

2 **Make your lapbook. Find pictures or draw. Then write.**

Upcycling in my garden

1 Which things from Activity 1 can you upcycle for the garden?

_____

2 What can you make with these things?

_____

3 How can you make them pretty?

_____

Home-school link 📥 Tell your family about things you can upcycle at home.

19

1 Read and write.

| straight coin smile moustache special beard |

Hi Alice,

This is a photo of my little sister and me. We've both got [1] _straight_ , brown hair and brown eyes. My sister has got a big [2] _____. She hasn't got a [3] _____ but she has got a [4] _____ in this photo! Me, too! 😄 My [5] _____ thing is a pretty bracelet. My sister's special thing is an old [6] _____.

Bye!
Sara

2 (2.25) Read and circle. Then listen and check.

[1]**Would** / **Can** you like to go to the museum with me on Friday, Tim?

[2]**Sorry,** / **Please,** I don't understand. Can you say that again, [3]**sorry** / **please**?

Yes, of course. [4]**Would** / **Can** you like to go to the museum with me on Friday?

Yes, [5]**thank you** / **please**. I'd love to!

[6]**Would** / **Can** you like to come too, Anna?

No, [7]**thanks** / **please**. Sorry, I [8]**can** / **can't**.

3   Now invite your friend to do these activities.

| have a picnic / Saturday afternoon | | go to an upcycling party / Sunday morning |

| do a nature trail / Saturday morning | | buy a new sweater / Tuesday after school |

4   Listen and write *B* (Bella), *T* (Tom), *A* (Alex) or *S* (Mr Smith). Then act out.

Whose is that book? *It's mine.*

Mini-project

5 Think of a special person. Write and circle. Ask and answer.

Hi _____,
How are you? Thank you for your email about your special person.
My special person is _____.
He / She is very special to me.
He / She has got _____
and _____.
He / She hasn't got _____
but _____.
His / Her special thing is _____
_____. It's important to
_____
because _____.
Bye! _____

Time to shine!

6 Read and tick (✓). Tell your friend.

1 I can write about my friend's special thing and why it is important. ☐

2 I can ask and talk about things people have got. ☐

3 I can write an invitation to an exhibition about our things. ☐

4 I can ask questions and say who things belong to. ☐

My favourite song is in
Unit 1 ☐ Unit 2 ☐
My favourite story is in
Unit 1 ☐ Unit 2 ☐

7 Vote. Sing or act out.

3 City of the future

Let's review! PB p22

Think and match.

plastic   metal   glass   paper

cup   shelf   box   plate   bowl

Lesson 1 ➡ Vocabulary

1 Read and number.

☐ market   ☐ shopping centre   ☐ theatre   ☐ restaurant   ☐ stadium
☐ art gallery   ☐ funfair   ☐ swimming pool   ☐ ice rink   ☐1 hotel

2 Look at Activity 1 and write.

1 The s<u>wimming pool</u> is next to the f<u>unfair</u>_____.
2 The s_____ is next to the r_____.
3 The h_____ is behind the m_____.
4 The a_____ is behind the s_____.
5 The i_____ is next to the t_____.

Tell me!

Which places in your town or city are fun to visit?

Extra time? Which places do you often go to?

1   Listen and number. Then match. Listen again and check.

a □   **b** 1   **c** □   **d** □

1 I like going to the market   because it's exciting.

2 I love going to the stadium   because it's scary.

3 I don't like going to the ice rink   because it's fun.

4 I don't like going to the funfair   because it's cold.

2 Look and write. Then think and complete for you.

1 I <u>like going to</u> the _____ because it's interesting.

2 I _____ the _____ because it's huge.

3 I **like / don't like** _____ _____ because it's _____ .

4 I **like / don't like** _____ _____ because it's _____ .

5 I _____ because _____ .

I can shine!

Do you like going to the... ?

3 💬 Ask your friend. Then write.

(name) _____ likes going to the _____ because it's _____ .

He / She doesn't _____ the _____

because it's _____ .

_____ because _____ .

_____

Extra time? Write ten new words. Then compare your list with a friend.

1 Read and circle. Then number.

> 1 (watch) / visit a show   2 visit / watch an exhibition
> 3 watch / go to a restaurant   4 go on / visit a ride

 a
 b   1
 c
 d

2 Look and number.

 a
 b   1
 c
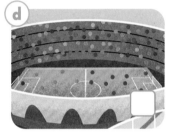 d

1 I've got an idea. Let's ride the bikes.

2 Do you like going to the stadium, Hugo?

3 Wow! I can see the exhibition!

4 What's this, Eva? How does it work?

I can shine!

Let's imagine!
What do you think? The story is:
OK ☆   good ☆☆   great ☆☆☆

3 What do you like doing? Tick (✓) or cross (✗). Then complete for you.

☐ watching a show at the theatre

☐ watching a match at the stadium

☐ visiting an exhibition at the art gallery

☐ going shopping at the market

I _____ watching a show at the theatre.

I _____ visiting an exhibition at the art gallery.

_____ a match at the stadium.

_____ at the market.

_____ but _____.

Extra time? Which free time activities do you often do?

Let's build!
Look at the photos in Activity 1. Ask and answer.

1 Look and write.

 ✓

 ✓

 ✗

1 Do you _like_ watching a show?
Yes, I do.

2 _____ like going shopping?
_____

3 _____
visiting an exhibition?
_____

 ✗

 ✓

4 _____ a restaurant?
_____

5 _____ ?
_____

2 Look, think and write. Then listen and check.

 museum ➡

 stadium ⬆

⬅ hotel

1 A: Excuse me. Where's the museum?
   B: Turn _right_ .

2 A: _____
   Where's the stadium?
   B: Go _____ .

3 A: _____
   the hotel?
   B: _____

I can shine!

3 Draw five places on the map. Then imagine you are at X. Ask and answer.

Excuse me. Where's the theatre ?

Go straight on. Then turn left... .

Pronunciation Say *excuse*. Which words have the same 'u' sound? fur turn huge cute curly

1 **Read and match.**

a I like going to the market because it's lovely.

b Olivia loves going to the swimming pool because it's clean.

c I don't like going to the square because it's dirty.

d Jack doesn't enjoy going to the theatre because it's boring.

4

☐

☐

☐

2 **3.18** **Listen and number. Then write. Listen again and check.**

| dirty   clean   lovely   ~~boring~~ |

a The theatre is __boring__ .   1

b The swimming pool is _____ .   ☐

c The market is _____ .   ☐

d The city square is _____ .   ☐

How can we keep our schools clean?

3 **Write about your town or city.**

I love going to the _____ because it's _____ .

I don't like going to the _____ because _____ .

My _____ likes going to the _____ because _____ .

He / She doesn't enjoy going to the _____ because _____ .

He / She _____ .

Extra time? Is your city clean? Tell your friend.

1 Read and circle.

1 Peter (likes) / doesn't like visiting an exhibition.

2 He **likes / doesn't like** going shopping.

3 Emily **likes / doesn't like** going shopping.

4 They **like / don't like** going on a ride at the funfair.

60%

Hi Katya,

How are you? I'm fine. Emily and I can't wait to see you next weekend.
What do you like doing? I enjoy visiting an exhibition but my sister Emily doesn't like going with me. She says it's boring. She likes going shopping but I think the shopping centre is boring! We both love going on a ride at the funfair because it's exciting! Tell me what you like doing and I can plan our weekend.
See you next weekend!

From Peter

---

2 Give it a go 💬 Where do you like going? Complete for you. Then ask and answer.

	You	Your friend
the ice rink		
the funfair		
the market		
the shopping centre		
watch a show		
visit an exhibition		
_____		
_____		

Do you like going to the funfair?

Yes, I do.

No, I don't.

I can shine! ✴

3 Write your email. Use Activities 1 and 2 to help you.

60%

Hi _____,

I can't wait to see you next weekend! What activities do you like doing?

I like _____

_____

_____

_____

See you next weekend!

From _____

Check your work! Check your full stops, exclamation marks and question marks.

1 **Think and write.**

1 This town isn't dirty. It's c_lean_ .

2 When you go on holiday, you can stay in a h_____.

3 She likes watching a m_____ at the s_____.

4 I like going shopping at the shopping c_____.

5 You can visit an exhibition at the art g_____.

6 You can go swimming in the swimming p_____.

7 He doesn't like going skating at the ice r_____.

2 🎧 3.21 **Listen and draw. Then write.**

Fred

1 Fred likes _watching a show_ .

2 He _____ going _____.

3 Does he _____ watching a _____?

4 Alison _____ going _____.

5 She _____ _____.

6 Does she _____ _____?

Alison

3 💬 **Look, ask and answer.**

> *Excuse me. Where's the theatre?*

> *Go straight on. The theatre is next to the shopping centre.*

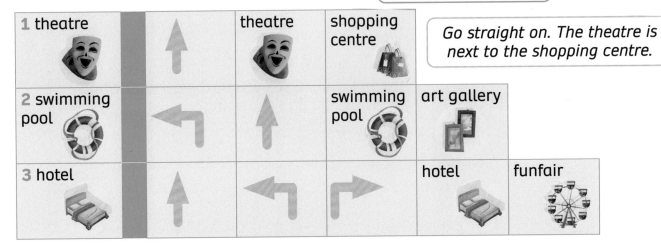

Extra time? Check your spelling. Order the letters and write.
lyolev   trathee   natresurat   ixinethibo

1 ✏️ **Think and write.**

Places in a city

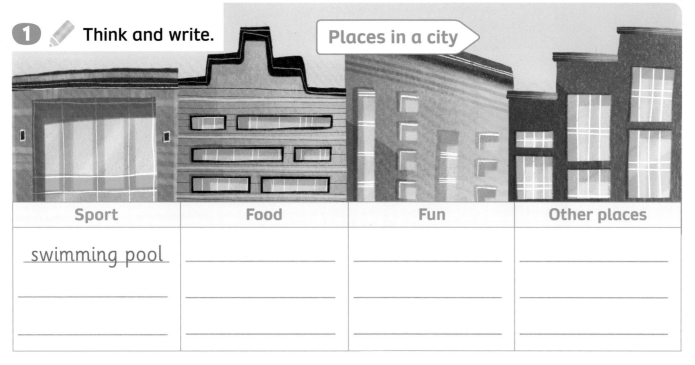

Sport	Food	Fun	Other places
swimming pool	_____	_____	_____
_____	_____	_____	_____
_____	_____	_____	_____

2 Make sentences about the places in Activity 1. Use these words.

boring   lovely   dirty   clean

The swimming pool is clean.

3 Make your lapbook. Find pictures or draw. Then write.

My dream city

1 Which places do you want in your dream city? _____

2 Which places do you like going to? Why? _____

3 Which places don't you like going to? Why? _____

Home-school link 🔽 Tell your family about places you like and don't like in your city.

29

Food for everyone!

Let's review! PB p34

Think and match.

1 watch   2 go on   3 visit   4 watch

a show   an exhibition   a ride   a match

Lesson 1 ➡ Vocabulary

1 **Read and number.**

	apples		flour		pineapples		honey		rice
1	sugar		potatoes		beans		lemons		grapes

2 **Look at Activity 1 and write.**

Fruit	Vegetables	Other
grapes		

Tell me!
What food can you buy at the supermarket?

30

Extra time? What fruit do you like?

1 (4.06) **Listen, read and tick (✓). Then write.**

There	is some	✓				
	are a lot of					
	isn't any					
	aren't many					

1 There's __some__ flour.

2 There isn't _____ sugar.

3 There _____ honey.

4 _____ apples.

5 _____ lemons.

2 **Look, circle and write. Compare with a friend.**

1 There **is** / **are** a lot of __apples__ .

2 There **isn't** / **aren't** many _____ .

3 There **is** / **are** some _____ .

4 There **isn't** / **aren't** many _____ .

5 There **isn't** / **aren't** any _____ .

3

1

4

2

5

I can shine!

3 **What's in your lunch box? Write. Use the words or your own ideas.**

cheese sandwich   pizza   fruit   salad   grapes   biscuits   apple   juice

There's a __cheese sandwich__ and there are a lot of _____ .

There are _____ but there aren't any _____ .

There's _____ but there isn't any _____ .

Extra time? Put new words into categories. This can help you remember the words.

31

1 (4.09) **Read and circle. Then listen and check.**

1 a **bag** / **bottle** / **piece** of orange juice

2 a **cup** / **piece** / **bottle** of fruit

3 a **glass** / **bag** / **bottle** of green apples

4 a **cup** / **box** / **bag** of hot chocolate

5 a **piece** / **bag** / **bottle** of flour

2 **Read the story again. Then think and write.**

good	~~waste~~	draw	many

1 They don't ~~throw away~~
   __waste__ any food!

2 There are a lot of _____
   strawberries.

3 Let's design _____
   a rainbow fruit salad!

4 The rainbow fruit salad is very
   tasty _____!

I can shine!

Let's imagine!
What do you think? The story is:
OK ☆   good ☆☆   great ☆☆☆

3 **Imagine you are a chef. Think and write.**

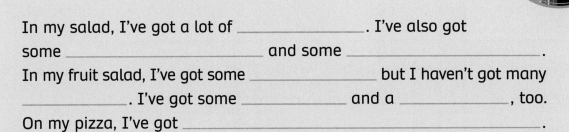

In my salad, I've got a lot of _____ . I've also got
some _____ and some _____ .
In my fruit salad, I've got some _____ but I haven't got many
_____ . I've got some _____ and a _____ , too.
On my pizza, I've got _____ .

Extra time? Name foods that are red, yellow, green or white.

1 **Look and write.**

1 **A:** Is there ___any___ juice?

B: Yes, __there is__ .

2 **A:** Are there _____ pieces of fruit?

B: No, _____ .

3 **A:** _____

boxes of _____ ?

B: _____

4 **A:** _____

a _____ ?

B: _____

Let's build!
What can you see in the photos in Activity 1?

I can shine!

2 💬 **Complete one side of the menu. Ask and answer.**

Kid's menu

Mains

potato salad $ _____

cheese burger $ _____

pizza $ _____

Drinks and snacks

pineapple juice $ _____

bottle of water $ _____

chocolate biscuits $ _____

How much is / are... ?

It's / They're... .

Pronunciation Say. Then circle the odd word out: brown owl flower sister town cow

1 **Read, think and complete.** | lemonade   smoothie   cake   ~~chips~~ |

CAFÉ EUROPA NO-WASTE MENU

| potatoes |
| 1 ___chips___ €1.50 |

| flour, eggs, butter, sugar |
| 2 _____ €2.50 |

| lemons, sugar, water |
| 3 _____ €2.00 |

| pieces of fruit, juice |
| 4 _____ €3.00 |

2 🎧 (4.18) **Listen and circle.**

Ben is making a cake with some ¹**apples /** (**flour**) and some
²**grapes / pineapples**. He can make a smoothie with some ³**carrot juice / apple juice**. He can also make some lemonade with some ⁴**lemons / pineapples** and some ⁵**honey / sugar**.

3 🎧 (4.19) **Circle the things Ben hasn't got. Then listen again and check.**

| rice | | flour | | beans | | grapes |

4 **Look, circle and write.**

I've got **a / an /** (**some**) grapes and I've got
a / an / some _____ .

I've got **a / any / some** _____
but I haven't got **a / an / some / any**

_____ .

I can make **a / an / some** _____ .

Do you waste any food at home?

Extra time? How can your family not waste food? Make a list.

1 Read and circle.

My no-waste party shopping list for 12 people

1 2 **honey** / (**chicken**) pizzas

2 1 **bag** / **glass** of potatoes
   (for chips)

3 1 box of **ugly** / **dirty** fruit
   (for fruit salad)

4 12 **huge** / **little** cakes

5 1 **box** / **cup** of biscuits

6 2 **pieces** / **bottles** of
   lemonade

2 Give it a go 💬 Write a no-waste party menu. Then ask and answer.

Food	Drink
_____	_____
_____	_____
_____	_____

*What do you want to eat /
drink at your party?*

*I want to eat… .
I want to drink… .*

I can shine! ✳

3 Write the shopping list for your
no-waste party. Then complete.

For _____ people

What do you want?	How many / much?
strawberries	1 big box
_____	_____
_____	_____

Food:
I want ___one big box of___
___strawberries___ and some
_____.
I also want _____ and
_____.
I don't _____
or _____.

Drink:
I want _____.
_____.
I don't _____
at my party.

Check your work! Check your spelling: beans potatoes strawberries

1 **Think and write.**

A ¹... of hot chocolate is nice on a cold day.

I enjoy eating a ²... of fruit.

I need to cut some ³... to make chips.

⁵... grow in hot countries.

I can make a cake with ⁴... , ⁶... , butter and eggs.

Bees make ⁷... .

You can put shopping in a paper or plastic ⁸... .

¹C	U	²P	

³

⁴ ... O ...

⁵ ... ... ⁶

U

⁷ ... E ...

⁸ ... ...

2 (4.22) **Write the questions. Then listen and write the answers.**

1 Is __there any__ rice? _____

2 Are _____ beans? _____

3 _____ tomatoes? _____

4 _____ cheese? _____

3 (4.23) **Listen again and write.**

1 There _____isn't any_____ rice.

2 There _____ beans.

3 There _____ tomatoes.

4 There _____ cheese.

4 💬 **Think and write. Then ask and answer.**

In my no-waste café, there are some _____ and some _____ .

How _____ is / are the _____ ?

It's / They're _____ .

Thank you.

Extra time? Which money do they use in the UK, the USA and your country?

1 🖊 **Think and write. Use the words or your own ideas.**

apples   carrots   rice   pineapples   ~~flour~~   sugar   honey   beans   potatoes

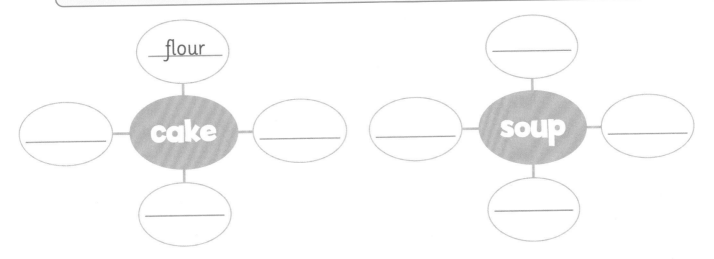

_____ — cake — _____

flour

_____

_____ — soup — _____

_____

_____

2 **Make your lapbook. Find pictures or draw. Then write.**

My no-waste recipes

1 Which are your favourite dishes? _____

2 Which dishes do you think you can make? _____

3 What do you need for these dishes? _____

_____

Home-school link ⬇ Ask your family about their favourite foods. Are yours the same or different?

37

Review 2 Our community

1 Read and write.

any lot aren't Are many are ~~there~~ some Is

1 A: Is <u>there</u> a cup of hot <u>chocolate</u>
   (telococha)?
   B: Yes, there is.

2 A: Are there any _____
   (stotepoa)?
   B: No, there _____ .

3 A: _____ there any _____
   (kecas)?
   B: Yes, there are but there aren't
   _____ !

4 A: Are there any cold drinks?
   B: Yes, there _____ . There are two
   _____ (ehomostis).

5 A: _____ there any fruit?
   B: Yes, there is. There are a _____
   of _____ (sperag) and
   there are _____ pineapples.

6 A: Is there _____ rice?
   B: Yes, there is. There's a _____
   (agb) of rice.

2 🎧 (4.25) 💬 Think and write. Then listen and check. Ask and answer.

Excuse me. ¹<u>How much</u> is
this bag of lemons?

² _____ £2.

Excuse me.
³ _____
the shopping centre?

Turn ▶ ⁴ _____ here. Then
◀ ⁵ _____ at the theatre, then
▲ ⁶ _____ .

3 Read, number and complete.

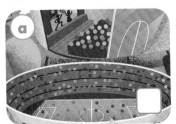   

1 A: What do you like ___doing___?
   B: I like going to the ___ice rink___
   because it's cool. I love skating!

2 A: What do you like _____?
   B: I like going to the _____
   to watch a football match.

3 A: Do you like going to the
   _____?
   B: No, _____. I think
   going shopping is boring.

4 A: Is there a good _____ in
   the town?
   B: No, _____ but there are
   some good cafés.

Mini-project

4 Imagine you are visiting your favourite city. Think and write.

Hi _____,

I'm visiting _____.
It's great! There are a lot of
_____ and
_____. I like going to
the _____ because
it's _____. I don't like
_____
because _____.

See you soon!

_____

Time to shine!

5 Read and tick (✓). Tell your friend.

1 I can write about things I like doing and places I like going in my town. ☐

2 I can write a shopping list with food and drink I need for a party. ☐

3 I can ask for and give directions to places in a town. ☐

4 I can ask and talk about how much food and drink there is. ☐

My favourite song is in
Unit 3 ☐ Unit 4 ☐

My favourite story is in
Unit 3 ☐ Unit 4 ☐

6 👥 Vote. Sing or act out.

Help our oceans!

Let's review! PB p42–43

Think and write.

| apples | sugar | honey |
| lemons | beans | flour |

(apples and flour crossed out)

apples _____

flour _____

Lesson 1 ➡ Vocabulary

1 Read and number.

- ☐ shark
- ☐ crab
- ☐ jellyfish
- ☐ dolphin
- ☐ starfish
- 1 whale
- ☐ octopus
- ☐ seal
- ☐ snail
- ☐ seahorse

Tell me!
Which sea animals have got legs? Which sea animals haven't got any legs?

2 Think and write.

1 s h a r k

2 d_____

3 s_____

4 c_____

5 j_____

6 s_____

7 o_____

8 s_____h

Extra time? Name four sea animals beginning with *s*.
Can you name any other animals beginning with *s*?

1 🎧 (5.06) **Write the words. Then listen and circle.**

1 The ___dolphins___ (hilponds) (are) / **aren't** playing in the sea.

2 The _____ (bracs) **are** / **aren't** climbing on the rocks.

3 The _____ (helaws) **are** / **aren't** singing.

4 The _____ (khasrs) **are** / **aren't** hiding behind the plants.

5 The _____ (sales) **are** / **aren't** dancing in the sea.

6 The _____ (asehseros) **are** / **aren't** swimming in the plants.

2 **Look and write. Then play a game.**

1 The jellyfish are
___swimming___. (swim)

2 The starfish aren't
_____. (jump)

3 The seahorses
_____. (hide)

*They're sleeping.
They aren't eating.*

Octopuses!

4 The octopuses
_____. (eat)

5 _____
_____ (climb)

I can shine!

3 **Look at Activity 2. Write.**

The _____ are _____ but they aren't _____.

The _____ _____ but they _____.

The _____ _____ but they _____.

Extra time? Write difficult words and easy words in different colours.

1 Look, think and write.

have   tell   recycle   clean   ~~make~~   pick up

1 <u>make</u> a film

2 _____ a beach clean up

3 _____ people

4 _____ rubbish

5 _____ the oceans

6 _____ rubbish

2 Read the story again. Then think and match.

1 Sofia [d]   **2** Zoe ☐   **3** Marco ☐   **4** Hugo ☐   **5** Eva ☐   **6** Socks ☐

a make a poster

b tell our friends

c have a beach clean up

d make a film

e help the children

f go to the beach clean up, too

I can shine!

Let's imagine!
What do you think? The story is:
OK ☆   good ☆☆   great ☆☆☆

3 Imagine you are planning a beach clean up.
Choose three things to do. Write.

My plan for a beach clean up
1 _____
2 _____
3 _____

Extra time? Compare your beach clean up plan with a friend.

1 Look, think and write.

1 Are they __picking up__ rubbish?

Yes, they __are__.

2 Are they _____ a film?

Yes, _____.

3 _____ recycling _____?

No, _____.

4 _____

a beach clean up?

_____

Are they picking up rubbish?

Number one!

Yes, they are.

Let's build!
Look at the photos in Activity 1. What are they doing? Play.

I can shine!

2 Today is Sunday. Ask and answer about the *Our oceans* event.

Our oceans weekend timetable

	Saturday	Sunday
10.00	*Our beautiful oceans* exhibition Ocean explorers' club	*Starfish* film cinema
2.00	*Clean oceans* film cinema	Talk about dolphins theatre
4.00	Talk about jellyfish theatre	Whale trail Ocean explorers' club

Excuse me. When is the talk about dolphins?

It's today. It starts at two o'clock.

When was the Clean oceans *film?*

It was on Saturday. It was at two o'clock.

Pronunciation Say *beaches*. Circle the words with the same sound at the end:
princes seahorses whales sandwiches grapes dresses

1 **Read, look and number.**

①  ②  ③  ④

a   Rubbish makes the beach dirty.   3

b   It's a plastic bag. ☐

c   This beach is very clean. ☐

d   There's rubbish on the beach. It's terrible! ☐

e   They're cleaning up the beach. ☐

f   It's safe for animals and people. ☐

g   It's a brilliant idea! ☐

h   It's very dangerous for sea animals. They can eat it! ☐

2 🎧 5.19   **Listen and number. Then write. Listen again and check.**

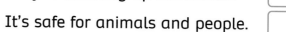
safe   ~~terrible~~   dangerous   brilliant

☐   Plastic is very _____ for animals and fish.

1   Oh, that river looks _terrible_ !

☐   That's a _____ idea!

☐   They want a _____ river in the future.

How much plastic do you think is in our oceans?

3 **Look, think and write.**

1   There's a lot of ¹ _rubbish_ in the park. The rubbish is very
² _____ for children.

I've got a ³ _____ idea! Let's
⁴ _____ up the rubbish.

2   There's / There are some ¹_____
in the ²_____ .

The ³_____ is / are ⁴_____ .

I've got a ⁵_____ idea! Let's
⁶ _____ .

Extra time? Which sea animal do you think is the same size as you?

1 **Read and circle.** *True* **or** *false*?

1 The film is called *Clean oceans*. **(T)** **F**

2 It's about plastic rubbish in rivers. **T** **F**

3 It's at two o'clock on Sunday. **T** **F**

4 You can buy tickets at the
information desk. **T** **F**

5 The film is in March. **T** **F**

Clean oceans

Plastic bottles and plastic bags are terrible for our beautiful oceans.
How can we help the sharks, sea turtles and starfish?
Come and watch this film!

Tickets:
£3 from the information desk
When?
2.00 p.m. Saturday 5th May
Where?
Ocean Museum, cinema

2 Give it a go **Imagine a film about sea animals. Make notes.**

What is the name of the film? _____

What is the film about? _____

Where can you see the film? _____

Which day is the film? _____

What time does it start? _____

I can shine!

3 **Make a film poster.**

Come and see

_____

Tickets: _____

When? _____

Where? _____

Check your work! Check capital letters for the names of days of the week, months and place names.

1 **Think and write. What's the word in the box?**

| 1 | j | e | l | l | y | f | i | s | h |

2

3

4

5

6

7

8

1 jeshilfly

2 tocsoup

3 brac

4 khars

5 keam a limf

6 kipc pu hubribs

7 leas

8 helaw

2 (5.22) **Listen and tick (✓). Then write.**

1

A: These children are at the ¹ <u>beach</u> .

B: ² _____ they doing?

³ _____ swimming?

A: Yes, ⁴ _____ .

2

A: These children are on the ¹ <u>rocks</u> .

B: ² _____ they ³ _____?

⁴ _____ looking at ⁵ _____?

A: No, they aren't. They're ⁶ _____

_____ .

3 💬 **Think and write. Then ask and answer.**

A: Excuse me. ¹ <u>Where's</u> the ocean film?

B: It's ² _____ . (place)

A: ³ _____ ? (day)

B: It's on ⁴ _____ .

A: ⁵ _____ ? (time)

B: It starts at ⁶ _____ .

Extra time? Which sea animal am I? My 1st letter is in *rice*, my 2nd letter is in *fur*, my 3rd letter is in *bag* and my 4th letter is in *box*.

1 💬 **Think and write. Then tell your friend.**

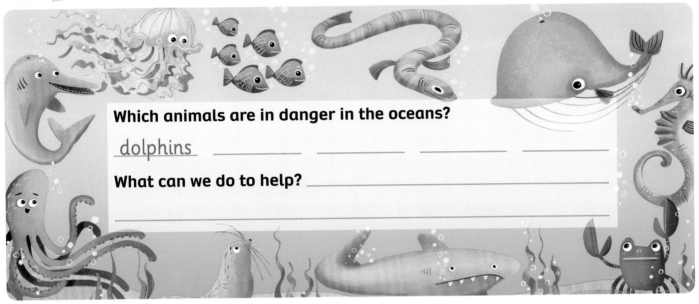

Which animals are in danger in the oceans?

<u>dolphins</u> _____ _____ _____ _____

What can we do to help? _____

_____

2 **Make your lapbook. Find pictures or draw. Then write.**

My beautiful ocean

1 Make a list of problems in the oceans. _____

2 How can you help? _____

3 Why is a clean ocean important for animals and people? _____

_____

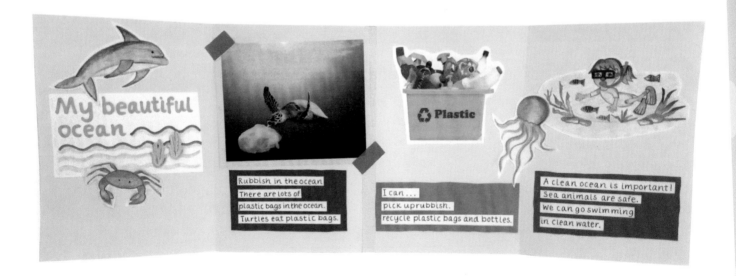

Home-school link 📥 Tell your family about how we can all help our oceans.

6 Let's play together!

Let's review! PB p54–55

Which animals have tails? Think and circle.

jellyfish (dolphin) shark whale octopus
seahorse seal crab starfish snail

Lesson 1 ➡ Vocabulary

1 **Read and number.**

| 1 | gymnastics | | baseball | | basketball | | swimming | | table tennis |
| | volleyball | | snowboarding | | hockey | | athletics | | badminton |

2 💬 **Complete. Then tell your friend.**

Play...	Do...	Go...
badminton		

I enjoy playing badminton.

I don't like doing athletics.

Tell me!
Which sports can you play in a team?

Extra time? Which sports can you do in winter?

1 **Listen and write G (girl) or B (boy). Then read and match.**

     B

1 The boy is going to ⎯⎯⎯⎯⎯⎯⎯⎯⎯
2 The girl is going
3 The boy is not going to do
4 The boy is

a to play baseball.
b gymnastics.
c going to play volleyball.
d play table tennis.

2 **Look, think and write. Then listen and check.**

①  ②  ③  ④

1 I'm __going__ to play basketball.
2 I'm not _____ to go _____ .

3 I'm _____ to _____ .
4 I'm not _____ .

I can shine!

3 **Imagine the sports you are going to do this weekend.**
Complete. Then write.

	Saturday	Sunday
I'm going to… .		
I'm not going to… .		

On Saturday, I'm going to _____
but I'm not _____ .
On Sunday, I'm going to _____
but I'm not _____ .

Extra time? Trace the name of a sport in the air. Your friend writes the word. Then check.

1 **Think and write.**

jump   run   win   throw   ~~hit~~   bounce

1 _hit_ a ball

2 _____ hurdles

3 _____ a ball

4 _____ a ball

5 _____ a race

6 _____ a race

2 **Read the story again. Then number.**

We can help you. ☐

I can do it! ☐

It's a team race. 1

We're first! ☐

Here you go, Marco! ☐

I'm not good at sport. ☐

I can shine!

Let's imagine!
What do you think? The story is:
OK ☆   good ☆☆   great ☆☆☆

3 💬 **Plan a race with four sports activities. Write.**
Then tell your friend.

I'm going to _____.

Then I'm going to _____.

I'm _____.

_____

I'm going to bounce a basketball.

Extra time? Mime and guess different actions in a race with your friend.

1 **Look, think and write.**

1 A: Are you going to <u>play baseball</u>?   2 A: _____ to play badminton?
   B: Yes, <u>I am</u>.   B: No, _____ . I'm going to _____ .

3 A: What _____ to do?   4 A: What _____ to do?
   B: I'm _____ a race.   B: I'm _____ .

I can shine!

Let's build!
What are you going to do this Saturday?

2 **Which sports do you like? Tick (✓) or cross (✗).**

snowboarding ☐   badminton ☐   volleyball ☐   athletics ☐   swimming ☐

3  **Write two sports in your diary. When are you free? Ask and answer.**

	Morning	Afternoon	Evening
Saturday			
Sunday			

Are you free on Saturday afternoon?   *Yes, I am.*

Do you want to play football?   *Yes, please! See you then.*

Pronunciation Say *thank you.* Circle the words with the same 'th' sound:
theatre   brother   smoothie   birthday   Maths   feathers

1 **Look and number. Then write.**

well badly can quickly ~~is~~ well

①  ②

a Our team ___is___ winning the match. We are playing _____. 2

b He isn't bouncing the ball slowly. He's catching the ball _____! ☐

c They aren't playing football _____. They're playing _____! ☐

d You _____ bounce the ball but you mustn't kick the ball! ☐

2 🎧 6.18 **Listen and tick (✓). Then read and circle. Listen again and check.**

ⓐ  ☐ ⓑ  ☐ ⓒ  ☐

Girl: I'm going to ¹**go snowboarding / play table tennis / play basketball**
on ²**Tuesday / Thursday** afternoon.

Boy: I can't ³**bounce / hit** the ball ⁴**well / badly** but I can ⁵**throw / catch**
the ball ⁶**well / badly**.

Do you like being in a team? Why? / Why not?

3 **Think and write for you.**

1 I can swim ___well___.

2 I can climb _____.

3 I _____ a ball _____.

4 I _____ well.

5 I _____ badly.

6 I _____.

Extra time? How many sports can you name? Make a list.

1 Read and answer the questions.

Hi Holly,

I'm going to play kayak baseball at the water sports centre next Saturday. You play in the swimming pool. It looks brilliant!

Are you free on Saturday morning? Do you want to play, too?

The water sports centre is on West Street. Kayak baseball is from ten o'clock to twelve o'clock.

I hope you can come!

Bye, Will

1 What's the name of the sport?
   <u>kayak baseball</u>
2 Why is this sport unusual?
   You play _____.
3 Which day is Will going to do it?
   _____
4 What time is he going to do it?
   From _____ to
   _____.
5 Where is Will going to do it?
   _____
   _____

2 Give it a go Imagine an unusual water sports event. Complete.

What sport is it? _____

Why is it unusual? _____

Which day are you going to do it? _____

What time are you going to do it? _____

Where are you going to do it? _____

I can shine!

3 Write a message to a friend about your unusual water sports event.
Use your notes in Activity 2.

Hi _____,

Do you like _____? I love _____ because

_____.

Are you free on _____? I'm going to _____.

It's on at _____ o'clock. It is at _____.

I hope you can come! Bye, _____

Check your work! Check: I'm, it's, o'clock

53

1 **Think and write.**

1 This game is big in the USA. You hit a small ball. b _aseball_

2 This game has got six people on each team. v_____

3 You use a special table to play this game. t_____

4 In basketball, you must b_____ the ball. You mustn't hit it!

5 You must run q_____ to win a race.

6 This word is the opposite of quickly. s_____

2 🎧 6.21 **Look and write. Then listen and check.**

Time	Saturday	Sunday
morning		
afternoon		

A: What ¹ _are you going_ to do on Saturday?

B: ² _____ to play badminton. Then I'm ³ _____ to the swimming pool.

A: Are ⁴ _____ to go swimming?

B: Yes, ⁵ _____ . ⁶ _____ swim in a race!

3 💬 **Look at Activity 2. Think and write. Then ask and answer.**

A: Are you free on ¹ _Sunday_ ?

B: Yes, ² _____ ! / No, ³ _____ .

A: Do you want to ⁴ _____ ?

B: Yes, ⁵ _____ ! ⁶ _____ then! / No, ⁷ _____ .

Extra time? It's a team sport. You don't bounce the ball. You play it at the sports centre or on the beach.

1 **Think and write. Use the activities or your own ideas. Then tell your friend.**

> doing gymnastics   going snowboarding   throwing a ball
> playing badminton   playing hockey   going swimming
> jumping hurdles   hitting a ball   doing athletics   running a race

I enjoy... _playing hockey_ ___

___

___

I'm good at... ___

___

___

My sports

I like watching... ___

___

___

I would like to try... ___

___

___

2 **Make your lapbook. Find pictures or draw. Then write.**

My sports

1 Which sports do you do now? ___

2 Which sports do you enjoy doing? Are you good at them? ___

___

3 Which sports would you like to try? Why? ___

4 Which sports do you enjoy watching? ___

Home-school link ⬇ Tell your family about your favourite sports.

55

1 Read and write.

Hi Donna,

What are you going to do this summer? I'm going to go to the ¹___Octopus___ (pucOtos) Summer Beach Camp on 5th July. It's £250 for one week.

I'm going to play team sports like ²_____ (skabbleat). I can ³_____ (uncobe) a ball very ⁴_____ (ewll) and I can run ⁵_____ (uciqykl)! I'm going to love it!

I'm also going to look for ⁶_____ (frashist) in rock pools. And I'm going to ⁷_____ (lecan) up the beach and make a film about our camp. The Octopus Summer Beach Camp is going to be ⁸_____ (tanrillib)!

Bye!
Carlos

2 🎧 6.23 💬 Listen and complete. Then match. Ask and answer.

1 Are you _free_ on Saturday?

2 Do you _____ to go to the beach clean up with me?

3 When _____ the beach clean up?

4 _____ is it?

5 What _____ does it start?

6 What time does it _____?

a It's on Saturday morning.

b It _____ at ten o'clock.

c _____, please! I'd love to.

d Yes, I am.

e It finishes at _____.

f It's on the beach, next to the café.

3 💬 Complete the sentences. Then ask and answer.

is doing   are playing   are   going to do   ~~What are~~   What is   are going to   doing

1 <u>What are</u> Marco and Hugo doing now?
2 They _____ volleyball.
3 What _____ Eva and Socks _____ on Friday evening?
4 They _____ watch TV.
5 _____ Zoe _____ now?
6 She _____ athletics with Sofia.

> What are Marco and Hugo doing now?   They are playing volleyball.

4 Read and complete. Use *was*, *wasn't*, *were* and *weren't*.
The beach clean up ¹_____was_____ a lot of fun and it ²_____ a lot of work.
It ³_____ a sunny day but it ⁴_____ hot. It was very cold! Emily and
Harry ⁵_____ at the beach. They were playing hockey. ⁶_____ you at the
clean up?

Mini-project

5 You are going to go to a summer camp. Think and write.

Hi _____,
What are you going to do this summer?
I'm going to go to the Octopus Camp in
_____.
It's €_____ for _____.
I'm going to play _____
_____ and _____.
I can _____ and
_____ well.
I'm going to _____
because it's _____. I'm not
_____ because
_____.
The camp is going to be brilliant!
Bye, _____

Time to shine! ✳

6 Read and tick (✓). Tell your friend.

1 I can write a film poster. ☐
2 I can write a message to a friend about a sports event. ☐
3 I can ask and answer questions about what people are doing now. ☐
4 I can ask and answer questions about what people are doing in the future. ☐

My favourite song is in
Unit 5 ☐   Unit 6 ☐
My favourite story is in
Unit 5 ☐   Unit 6 ☐

7 👥 Vote. Sing or act out.

 **from The Rise and Shine Museum**

1 Think and write.

| dolphins potatoes freckles funfair jacket | pretty ugly boring lovely |
| ice rink table tennis grapes seahorses sweater | dirty clean brilliant terrible |

I like...	because...	I don't like...	because...
my sweater	it's pretty.	going to the ice rink	it's boring.

2 (7.05) Think and write. Then listen and check.

1 The woman __hasn't__ got freckles.

2 The boy is going to go to the _____ for his birthday.

3 They're using _____ fruit to make a new dish.

4 People don't _____ their rubbish on the beach.

3 Read and match. Then ask and answer for you.

1 Is there a market   a go next weekend?

2 What do you like   b got a stadium?

3 Has your town   c in your town?

4 Where are you going to   d doing in your town?

4 Read and match.

 1 [ ]
 2 [a]
 3 [ ]
 4 [ ]
 5 [ ]
 6 [ ]

a   She's got straight, blonde hair. She likes going shopping.

b   He's got brown eyes and straight, brown hair.

c   She's got curly, black hair and a ponytail. She loves animals.

d   He's got green eyes and short, black hair. He thinks he isn't good at sports but he is!

e   He lives in the museum. He likes sleeping in a box.

f   She works in the museum. She's got a special bracelet.

5 Make your lapbook. Find pictures or draw. Then write.

My favourite things in the Rise and Shine Museum

1   My favourite character in the Rise and Shine Museum story is _____.

2   I like him / her because he / she _____.

3   My favourite new words are _____, _____, _____ and _____.

4   My favourite story is _____.
    I like it because _____.

5   I like the song from Unit _____ because _____.

6   Now I can talk about _____.

Home-school link 📄 Tell your family about the Rise and Shine Museum.

59

Museum Takeover Day

1 **Look and write. Then imagine, point and say.**

~~welcome~~ help cook
clean plan work

1 <u>welcome</u> visitors

2 _____ as
a tour guide

3 _____ the
museum

4 _____
an exhibition

5 _____ in
the museum shop

6 _____ in the
museum café

2   **Match. Then listen and check.**

*I enjoy talking to people.
I want to welcome visitors.*

It's Museum Takeover — we play!
Children — Day,
We help, we cook, — do everything!
And then, of course, — we clean, we plan,

World Food Day

3   **Think and write. Then listen and check.**

1 We <u>should</u> eat
a <u>healthy</u> diet.

2 We _____ drink a
lot of _____ .

3 We _____ eat
junk _____ .

4 We _____ eat a lot
of fruit and _____ .

5 We _____ choose
_____ food.

6 We _____ eat a
lot of _____ .

International Day of Forests

4 🎧 💬 Look and tick (✓) or cross (✗). Then listen and check. Tell a friend.

> *We mustn't pick the flowers.*

5 **Think and write.**

1 We ___must plant___ trees.

2 We _____ the animals.

3 We _____ the gates.

4 We _____ on the paths.

5 We _____ rubbish.

6 We _____ the flowers.

Protect our forest

Key
✓ = must
✗ = mustn't

Museum Open Day

> *Would you like to play a game?*

> *Yes, I would! I'd like to play chess.*

6 **Write and match. Then ask and answer for you.**

a A: Would you like to _do a tour_
(od a rtou)?

B: No, I wouldn't. 〔2〕

b A: Would you like to draw a
_____ (retipuc)?

B: Yes, please. I _____!
I'd like to draw an old boat.

c A: Would you like to make a
_____ (delmo)?

B: Yes, _____. I'd _____
make a castle.

d A: _____ you like to play a
_____ (meag)?

B: No, I _____.

Word connections

Word connections key

 Places

 People

 Activities

 Things

 Ocean animals

 Food

Welcome

Visiting a museum

app
camera
exhibition
museum
museum director
phone

Our things

fun games
important photos
popular books
special toys

1 Who are we?

Describing people

beard
big eyebrows
blonde hair
curly hair
freckles

moustache
ponytail
smile
straight hair
wavy hair

What other words to describe people do you know? Add your words.

Special things

blanket
bracelet
coin
drum
earrings
necklace

2 Let's use it again!

Everyday things

bowl	plate
box	pot
cup	rug
handbag	shelf
jacket	sweater

What other everyday things do you know? Add your words.

Materials

glass
metal
paper
plastic
rubber
wood

3 City of the future

Places in a city

art gallery	restaurant
funfair	shopping centre
hotel	stadium
ice rink	swimming pool
market	theatre

What other places in a city do you know? Add your words.

Activities in a city

go on a ride
go shopping
go to a restaurant
visit an exhibition
watch a match
watch a show

4 Food for everyone!

Food

apples	lemons
beans	pineapples
flour	potatoes
grapes	rice
honey	sugar

What other food words do you know? Add your words.

Food containers

bag of rice
bottle of juice
box of fruit and vegetables
cup of hot chocolate
glass of water
piece of fruit

5 Help our oceans!

Ocean animals

crab   seal

dolphin   shark

jellyfish   snail

octopus   starfish

seahorse   whale

What other ocean animals do you know? Add your words.

Beach clean up activities

clean the oceans

have a beach clean up

make a film

pick up rubbish

recycle rubbish

tell people

6 Let's play together!

Sports

do athletics   play baseball

do gymnastics   play basketball

go snowboarding   play hockey

go swimming   play table tennis

play badminton   play volleyball

What other sports do you know? Add your words.

Sporting activities

bounce a ball

hit a ball

jump hurdles

run a race

throw a ball

win a race

What other sporting activities do you know? Add your words.